YOU MAY BE A BADASS BUT YOU NEED A PLAN

Will Edwards

PAPERBACK EDITION

The first part of this book was originally published (2011) under the title *The Making of a Warrior*. The second part was previously published (2018) as *You May be a Badass but You Need to Write*. This new edition of *You May be a Badass but You Need a Plan* (2019) includes the full text of both of the above works.

Revised Edition Published: March 2019

This book is provided for own your personal use. No portion of this book may be reproduced in any form except as permitted by U.S. copyright law. You may not change this book or distribute it without the prior, written permission of the publisher.

Copyright © White Dove Books 20011-19

Contents

PART 1 – THE ALLEGORY 4

THE DAY I MET ATIP 7

THE HATCHING OF A PLAN 12

THE SLOUGH OF DESPOND 16

TIME TO REFLECT 21

MY HOMEWORK 26

SAYING GOODBYE 29

REFLECTION 31

STUDY QUESTIONS 33

SUMMARY 38

PART 2 – MY NEW PLAN 40

WHAT YOU HAVE TO DO 43

ALGORITHMS 49

FINDING A MARKET 54

RESEARCHING YOUR BOOK 62

CREATING YOUR BOOK 67

YOUR BLURB 81

TRAFFIC 90

BUILDING YOUR EMPIRE 95

PUTTING IT TOGETHER 98

RESOURCES 104

FINALLY 107

MORE FROM WILL EDWARDS 109

ABOUT WHITE DOVE BOOKS..110

Part 1 – The Allegory

It was in the year 2000 when I first began trying to earn a living online. I remember reading, back then, about a bunch of college kids who had just sold their online business for millions of dollars. It was the height of the *dotcom* revolution and the bubble had not yet burst. At the time, nobody realised that there was a bubble, let alone that it was about to burst.

Over the years, I tried many things with varying degrees of success. I wasted a lot of money buying books on the subject of how to make money online and found very little in them that was of any real value. In addition, I tried a number of systems and courses and, in the process managed to get scammed out a couple of thousand dollars, and one program still owed me about $1,000 in unpaid commission when it went belly up.

Despite all of that, I persisted and began to do my own thinking. Eventually, I built a very successful website and my online income gradually increased until it was about equal to the income from my day job. Naturally, at that stage I quit, confident that I would be able to move things forward more quickly as I would be working on my web business full time.

But then, quite suddenly, things began to go seriously wrong. Google changed its ranking algorithms in a series of updates (known as *Panda*) that caused my site traffic to plummet. In the space of a few short months, visitors dropped from around 5,000 per day to about 100 people per day. And my income fell in direct proportion. It was a terrible shock. At that same time, my marriage fell apart. We spent months and months, the dog and me, walking together over the moor for long hours. It was a low point in my life; perhaps the lowest point. I couldn't work, I couldn't even think straight.

People were trying to tell me that I could rebuild my income by reworking the site. They were well-meaning but they didn't understand why I had been getting so much traffic. The fact is that my blog had many front page rankings for a myriad terms related to the subject of *personal development*. There was not just one page that would need to be fixed, there were thousands of them. It would have taken a huge amount of time and effort with no absolute guarantee of success.

But there was one overriding consideration that prevented me from trying to salvage the business model: even if I managed to get my traffic back again, what would protect me from the vagaries of the Google programmers? My business would always be one algorithm update away from failure. As far as I was concerned, Google and I had an unwritten arrangement: I provided good quality, original content on a daily basis and they sent me traffic. They reneged on the deal; I was not going to go through it again.

From that experience I learned a few hard lessons: firstly, the web is always changing and you need to stay ahead of the curve; secondly, being reliant upon Google for my prospects was a weak part of my business model. Life's lessons are sometimes difficult to learn.

That was two years ago.

After such a crushing experience, it would have been easy for me to give up on my dream of creating a 6-figure online income. That had always been my objective from the start, and I almost managed it too; I got to 5 figures in passive income before things fell apart. But, do you know something? Successful people always get up again and have another go; that's what separates them from the remainder.

So, after much deliberation, I decided to keep my website going and rework the business model. Let's face it, I had achieved online success where 95% of the people who tried had failed – some estimates suggest the figure is much higher. What I needed to do was re-examine what had worked for me and apply the same basic principles to a new venture. I needed to establish, specifically, what worked, and what I had actually done to create success. When I was clear about that, I would be ready to try again.

The following text tells of my journey from complete newbie to successful online marketer. My story is told as an allegory because I thought it would be fun to have a go at writing one.

The Day I Met Atip

Arriving at the gates of the Warrior's meeting place for the first time, I was aware of the subtle mixture of emotions within. There was definitely a bit of excitement mixed with some trepidation and at first, I wondered if it was even okay to go in.

The sign said 'Welcome', so I finally went inside and called out, in a not very convincing voice,

"Hello, I'm new here. Just wanted to say hi."

Before I knew it, someone had answered. It was Atip. He was very welcoming and was to become a kind of mentor to me over the coming years, but at the time I did not know that.

"Hi," he said "Welcome to the Warrior's Meeting Place. If there's anything you need, there are plenty of helpful people around here, so just ask and you are sure to get a good answer."

That's great, I thought, and I was just about to ask the first question that was on my mind, when someone else asked it for me.

"Hey," said Ankh "Can someone tell me how I can be successful?"

That saved me the bother, so I just sat down and waited for the Warriors to answer. What transpired was not, I guess, what either of us expected. Firstly, Pancake237 commented that Novice Warriors needed to start asking better questions. And then Tobias3rd added his comment to the effect that Ankh really needed to spend a bit of time reading through the archives.

Before long, quite a number of people commented, but I don't think Ankh was very impressed. He actually replied to one or two of those people. Something to the effect that he was only trying to learn and he thought he had come to the right place. But perhaps he was mistaken. Boy was I glad that I didn't ask that question.

After a brief period of reflection, I thought about what Tobias3rd had said about the archives. There must be some really good material in there, I thought. So I went off to the dungeon with my reading glasses and the intention of getting an education. After reading for quite a short while, the first thing I realised was that a lot of people had previously asked exactly same the question that Ankh had asked, and there were lots of answers to it right here in the archives. So Toabias3rd was right about reading the archives. I actually learned quite a lot from my sojourn there.

Once of the most important things I learned was how to recognise a true Warrior. You see, of all the people who had taken the time to answer this question in the past, every now and then you found someone who seemed to identify with the plight of the Novice. These people seemed to be encouraging, understanding and genuinely helpful. I made a mental note of some of those names and then, I had a little brainwave.

It was possible to search the archives in such a way as to find what these True Warriors had said in the past. That kind of stuff, I thought, should be well worth reading. So I dedicated myself to reading, learning and trying to understand this great problem of success. It was indeed an education. But I knew that there was a lot more to learn and, since a lot of questions had been asked repeatedly, I was beginning to see the same answers quite often. It was time to go back up to the main floor of the meeting place.

Back on the main floor, I wandered around listening to other people's conversations for a while. As it turned out, there were a lot of Novice Warriors asking similar questions. I could feel the smile on my face as I realised that I knew a lot of the answers thanks to my spell in the dungeon reading the archive material and I was just congratulating myself on my first achievement when I bumped into Atip.

"Hey, my man," said Atip "How's it going? You getting what you came here for?"

I began to tell Atip about my spell in the archives and how much I'd learned when he interrupted to say,

"Great, great! That's a really good start. You are probably now ready for some clarification, so are you ready to ask your first question?"

I thought for a moment, not sure of what that might be. Of course, thanks to Ankh, I certainly knew what it was not going to be. Then I asked Atip,

"Well, I was wondering exactly how to get started. Do you think that would be a good question to ask?"

Atip placed his finger alongside his ample nose in a contemplative manner and then replied,

"You know something? That question tells me something interesting about you. It tells me you are a person of action because you want to get started and that's really good. But you get the best answers to simple direct questions. You see, the problem with that question is that there are ... well, a million possible answers and ..."

"Oh come on," I couldn't help interrupting "a million answers?"

Atip sighed. After a brief pause, he asked me a question,

"How many people do you think there are enjoying the level of success you desire, right now? Have a think and try to put a number on it"

I thought.

"Well," I began "there are certainly lots of unsuccessful people out there. Lots of people who are trying to become successful ..."

"Lots? How many do you suppose?"

"I really don't know!"

Atip explained that about 95% of people fail to achieve outstanding success. He said he knew that by listening to a famous Warrior who's opinion he respected. And then he added there that are almost 7 billion people on the planet and if only 5% of them had achieved outstanding success, that's about a third of a billion people.

"Wow!" I was impressed.

He then said something that made me stop and think.

"So, that means there are about a third of a billion ways to become successful."

"But hold on there," I replied "they can't all be doing different things. There just can't be *that* many ways to become successful."

Atip scratched his nose as a grin began to form itself across his face.

"No," he said "You are right. There are probably a lot more than that!"

The Hatching of a Plan

After thinking about what Atip said about there being so many different ways to become successful, I began to realise that I had to find my own way, my own method. So I sat down with a blank sheet of paper and decided that I needed a plan. After staring at that paper for a while, I realised that I was not in a position to hatch my plan.

What should I do, I asked myself? Well, I knew the answer. What I would do is get myself over to the Warrior's meeting place to look at the plans that other Warriors had come up with. That way I would be able to get some inspiration. I knew from my spell in the archives that there were plans laying about all over the place.

When I began to look for plans, I found a lot that were quite similar. Then I thought back to what Atip had said. Hmm, if there were at least a third of a billion ways of becoming really successful, why were there so few plans? Now, you know what struck me? That's a good question! It's specific, it's direct and it's simple. The thought crossed my mind that perhaps I should ask it on the main Warrior floor. But then I thought I would save it to ask Atip when I next saw him.

Meanwhile, I began to get my plan together, which was an aggregation and distillation of several plans that I found laying about in the archives. I even began to tweak the plan myself, chucking in some bits and pieces of my own thinking here and there, all the time thinking to myself that this plan is going to work. I am going to become really successful. In fact, the more I planned, the more I thought that it was going to be really simple to achieve that success after all.

When I had finished my planning session, I felt really great, really pleased with myself, and the first thing I wanted to do was to show Atip and ask him what he thought about it. So I went right up to the Warrior main floor and looked for him, but to no avail. He was not there. For two days, I lurked about the place, coming and going, just waiting to bump into him again, but he was nowhere to be found.

Well, I really wanted the feedback that I knew Atip could provide before I started my plan, but as he was not about, I thought I would just start. I felt sure this plan was going to work, so perhaps I didn't need his input after all. For the next three days I worked flat out on my plan. Every day, I took a stroll around the Warrior floor hoping to bump into Atip, then on the fourth day, he was there.

"Hi Atip," I opened "I haven't seen you about lately."

"Yes," he replied "I have been quite busy working on my latest project."

This gave me a lovely warm feeling because I realised that he had been doing exactly what I had been doing. We had both been working on becoming successful.

"Me too!" I said. "Actually, I wanted to get your opinion on my plan, if you don't mind giving it, that is."

"You don't need my opinion," he answered.

"Well, I do understand if you are busy that you ..."

"No," he interrupted "you really don't need my opinion because your results contain the answer you are looking for. If your plan is good and you have been following through by taking action, then the results you expect should naturally follow."

"Yes, I realise that, but what if they don't?" I enquired.

"Then that's a good thing," he said "because you will know that your plan needs to be updated or thrown away."

He went on to explain that you have to start somewhere and, in the absence of having your own plan, taking someone else's and testing it to see if it actually works is a really smart move. He told me that the vast majority of people don't do that and so they don't get to know, from experience, what works and what doesn't.

"Let me ask you something," he said "how did you go about constructing that plan of yours?"

Now, I thought I had done a great job because I had not just simply copied someone's plan. I had combined what I thought were the best features from many different sources and added some of my own ideas. And – this is where I thought I had done a good job – I had selected from the material offered by the True Warriors I had previously identified when I searched the archives.

"You did a good job," he commented. "Now you just need to analyse your results and start the process of tweaking. Remember that: Plan, Do, Check, Tweak! If you keep doing that, you can't go wrong."

"But ... erm ... I need to know if my plan is any good," I eventually managed to stammer.

"That's right, you do. And the way to find out is to check your results. They are everything. Your results are the vindication of your methods. If you can measure your level of success, whatever it is right now, then you can work on improving it. And you remember how you can do that?"

"Tweaking?"

"Yes, tweaking. Keep tweaking based on the measurement of your results."

And he walked across the main floor and out of the concourse. As he mounted his horse, he waved and then rode off toward the distant hills.

Right at that moment, I thought again about that question I had meant to ask him, but it would have to wait until next time.

The Slough of Despond

Well, for the next few weeks, I didn't see Atip again. No doubt he was just too busy being successful himself. For all of that time, I had been working my plan. I remembered the old adage: you must first plan your work and then you must work your plan. And that is what I was doing, but I was also reflecting on what Atip had said, because he had gone a couple of steps further. He said that after the planning and the doing, needed to come the checking and tweaking.

So for those weeks, every day I was busy checking my results and plotting them on a graph to see if there was any progress I could identify. The results were pretty poor as far as I could see. Sure there was a little bit of success. But it was a lot harder to keep up the effort than I had first thought and the results were definitely not in direct proportion to the effort I was putting in, as far as I was concerned.

It was about then that I met Lazarus, one spectacularly sunny day, at the meeting place. He was very friendly and seemed to have lots of time to spare. He also seemed to know a lot about the subject of success. Right off the bat, he told me that my plan was rubbish. He said that he had tried doing exactly the same thing a couple of years ago and it just didn't work. How I wished I had bumped into him sooner. He could have saved me a lot of time, I thought.

"Lucky for you that you ran into me," he told me, "because I am a *Badass* at making money and pretty soon, you will be too!"

After a lot of chat about our respective experience, he suggested that I ought to get involved in a success program he was promoting. He was making a killing, he told me, and it was as easy as falling off a log. Someone as bright as me ought to be able to achieve the level of success I desired within a few short weeks. I kicked myself for wasting the past few weeks on my hair-brained plan and wished I had met this fellow sooner.

Within just a few minutes, I had enrolled in the same program as Lazarus. It looked really good. The website was very professional with lots of great tools and gizmos that I wondered how I thought it would be possible to manage without. And best of all, it was only costing me a mere $19 per month to be a privileged member. With all the great tools, I could see it was such a great deal that other people would be mad not to join and I could make 50% commission by referring other people.

So, now I knew exactly what to do. I tore up my original rubbish plan and was really pleased to have a new, workable plan. If it was working so well for Lazarus, it would work for me too, so I threw myself into promoting this new program. After a few weeks, I knew I would be, well perhaps not rich, but well on my way to success.

About a week later, I bumped into Atip again at the meeting place.

"Hey there," he said "How's that plan of yours going? You should have some decent stats now and be about ready to go into your tweaking phase."

"Oh yes," I replied "... erm ... well I figured I could save myself a lot of time by coming up with a better plan because, as it turned out, my plan was rubbish!"

"And how do you know that?" he asked.

"Well, I learned that the plan was rubbish by showing it to another Warrior," I answered. "He told me he had tried the same thing a couple of years ago and it just didn't work."

"I am disappointed at you," he remarked. "You didn't even go round the cycle once. How do you expect to achieve anything if you are not prepared to see things through?"

"Oh don't worry about me," I replied "I am a *Badass* and I have a much better plan now. I am working on it every day and it is sure to get me to where I want to be in just a few weeks."

"A *Badass*?"

His expression seemed to signal doubt.

"Well, good luck," he said. "Just remember what we discussed previously. Don't just listen to what others tell you without due consideration. Sure you can listen, but you have to begin to think in the right way too. Let your own results tell you whether or not your plans are any good."

As he made his way out of the concourse, I was left thinking about the situation I was in. Did I make a mistake abandoning my first plan too soon? It didn't take too much thinking about. There was no way I was prepared to bust a gut putting in all that effort for very little return. The new plan seemed to promise a much brighter future and I was going to give it my all.

For the next few months, I tried everything I could think of to make my new plan work, but nothing seemed to be working for me at all, at first. Still, I had access to an amazing array of tools and it had only cost me $57, so far. Surely it would only be a matter of time before this new plan began to pay off. Then, shortly after my third month of membership, something great happened: somebody saw one of my ads and bought into the same program as me.

Now, I was really happy because I knew I was going to be earning $9.50 per month from this one person's membership as my hard earned commission. I was feeling very good indeed. I only needed another 175 people to join up under me for me to be earning enough to quit my day job. I realised that other people might be put off, but I felt that it would simply be a matter of time. So I went at it with renewed vigour.

One month later, the other person left the program and I had no new sign-ups to show for all of my effort. I knew I was doing something wrong, but did not know what it could be. At about this time, I bumped into Lazarus again at the meeting place.

"Hi Laz," I began "How's it going with your membership? Are you still making loads of cash?"

"Glad you asked my friend," he said, "I am indeed making loads of dosh, but I dumped that program because it was not bringing in enough. Sure, I was making a killing with that program at first, but the market is now saturated. I have found another, much better program now. It earns me twice the commission and it takes less time to find the prospects because of a viral twist they have in the marketing funnel."

Well, I was relieved to hear that it was not my fault now he had told me what the problem was with the saturated market. How fortunate I had been to have bumped into him again, I thought.

"Hey," he added "this new program would suit you down to the ground. You could easily be pretty wealthy in just a few weeks doing this and it's really easy too. Do you want me to get the details over to you?"

"Let me think about it," I said, as that odd feeling of déjà vu came over me.

Time to Reflect

So, it was time to reflect on where I was and what would be the right way forward for me. I decided to leave the program because it had cost me exactly $76 and I had made a total of $9.50 in commission. So, as I was $66.50 down in hard cash, it was a really easy decision. I knew the program was not going to work for me because I had put in four months of solid effort and I had actually managed to lose money in the process.

Had not Atip told me this very thing before I got involved in that program? He said that the results needed to speak for themselves. That's how you would know whether a plan was good or not. As it turned out, my original plan was actually better than this 'promising' new program that Lazarus told me about. I also remember that Atip said that after the planning and doing, needed to come the checking and tweaking.

I had invested four months getting absolutely nowhere in that program. Where would I be right now, I asked myself, if I had committed that time to checking and tweaking? Somewhere, I remember someone saying, at one time, that your first loss is your best loss. Well, I don't know if that's the case or not, but what I do know is that the experience may have cost me $66.50, but I had learned something. I learned that sometimes you have to pay money in order to really learn a fundamental truth.

Was it time to dig my old plan out of the waste basket? I was not sure, after all, it did not seem to be as promising as I originally thought, but then again, I had not done the whole Plan, Do Check, Tweak cycle. At this stage, I felt I really needed to talk to Atip again, but meanwhile I would go and mix with the Warriors and see if I could pick up any more good ideas.

One day, I was chatting with another Warrior, named Searchah26, about his plans. He was telling me how he had a similar experience to me when he first started out, but he was now very philosophical about it, pointing out that what doesn't kill you makes you stronger. He said that he was now working on a plan to provide a *service* rather than a *product* and that he felt this was where his future direction lay.

I asked him what the difference was between a product and a service. He laughed and then, after a brief moment of contemplation answered.

"I would say, mainly, it is recurring income."

It got me thinking: I wonder what kind of service I might be able to offer?

As we were talking, another Warrior joined in. It was his first visit to the meeting place and he asked if it would be okay to ask a question to the other Warriors. I asked him what he wanted to know and he said he wanted to know how to succeed. I was about to tell him about the archives when, right then, Lazarus came up to the group and started talking about his new opportunity. As I began to tell Lazarus that I had decided not to get involved, I could see the new Novice was hooked and they walked off together talking about how easy it would be to get filthy rich.

As I began to walk away, I noticed the elegant black stallion tethered outside the concourse and realised that Atip was somewhere in the meeting place. A short search and I was able to find him.

"Hi Atip," I began "I wanted to say sorry for my lack of understanding of what you were trying to tell me when we last met."

Gracious as ever, Atip smiled and said,

"My friend, you don't need to apologise. It is only when the student is ready that the teacher can appear. Remember that you always need to be ready in order to move forward. You sometimes get the right information at the wrong time, and that's okay. Just remember the lesson."

"So I wanted to tell you that the second plan turned out to be rubbish," I said.

He lifted an eyebrow and leaned forward a little as he questioned, in a very confidential tone,

"And you found that out by doing and then checking the results – right?"

"Yes!" I replied.

"Then you have learned how to know whether your plan is a good one. Do you remember asking me that question? Now you have your own answer and notice that it came from within you. All the best answers come from within."

All of this time, since our last talk, I had been wanting to get that other question that I mentioned answered by Atip, so I thought that now would be a very good time to ask.

"When you first told me about tweaking, I remember just as you were riding off, thinking of a really good question I wanted to ask you. So I am really glad to be able to ask you now."

"I am all ears," he said.

"Now what was it?" I said, thinking out loud.

"Yes, that is a very good question," he replied.

"No, I remember now. If there are at least a third of a billion ways of becoming really successful, why do there seem to be so few plans?" I asked.

"That *is* a good question. But let me ask you one in return" he said. "After *you* have become successful, will you publish your plan for everyone else to read?"

"I don't know." I eventually answered "Possibly."

"That's a good answer. You may, but then again you may not. Successful people are busy being successful, not usually, explaining to others how to become successful. There are many plans to which you will never have access and that's why forming your own plan is so difficult to begin with."

"So, how do I start? I mean, how do I start creating a good plan?" I replied.

"Well," he said slowly and deliberately "you start by *not* starting. You don't start by constructing a plan, you start with a *strategy*. Between now and next time we meet, I would suggest that you start thinking about who you are trying to serve and what they need. Once you properly understand that, you can begin to come up with a plan to meet those wants and needs."

As I said the following words, "... but I already know who I am trying to help. My market is very broad and includes everybody between the ages of 16 and 80, of any level of education, belonging to any level of the social strata who might need to develop, in any one of a myriad ways, in order to achieve their true potential," I simultaneously realised how stupid they were.

He looked me in the eye and winked. He knew, of course that I'd realised there was some homework for me to do.

My Homework

To begin with, I decided to start researching the subject of *strategy* and why we need one, and I finally came up with some very good answers: we need a strategy because of the existence of *competition* and strategy is how we *win* the game.

Our strategy is how we *position* ourselves as the natural and logical provider of the goods or services our customer wants or needs in order to achieve their goals. Now all of this stuff is quite an eye-opener don't you think?

Before you can begin to think about positioning yourself as the natural and logical provider of goods or services, you first have to understand what your customer wants or needs in order to achieve *their* goals. That means you have to get deep into the heads of your target market and that, in turn, means that you need to know who they are, specifically, and what they are trying to achieve, in detail.

Now, in any market, there are existing suppliers of goods and services with whom we must compete. Their presence is a good thing because, if there is no competition, then there is no market. What we need to do is figure out how we can do better than the competition in some way. We need to provide better products or services, better marketing if we want to attract sales and affiliates and we need to support our customer's outcomes better.

So our strategy needs to encompass the following:

- We Need a Vision
- We Need a Plan
- We Need Unique Selling Propositions (USPs)

It took me a while, but eventually, I managed to identify who my target market was and what they were trying to achieve. Following that, I was able to identify various products and services I could provide and a way of doing so that would make me unique.

My plan came about by completing the following steps:

- Understand the Customer's Outcomes, Wants and Needs
- Decide on the Product(s) or Service(s) to Offer
- Develop or Acquire the Necessary Skills and Tools
- Develop the Vision, Mission and Plan

Once the new plan was formed, I immediately felt I wanted to get some feedback from Atip, but I realised that I already knew what he would say to me. He would tell me that there is only one way to find out whether or not the plan was a good one: Plan, Do, Check, Tweak – that was his formula for success.

So I resolved to complete the plan based upon my strategy of serving my target market in a way that firmly separated me from the competition.

By the time I met Atip again, I was resolved to have executed the first part of my plan so I would be ready to discuss the results with him. And, when I had completed the first part of my plan, I got immediate feedback. The results told me that the plan was going to work. This was not based upon any kind of estimation or gut-feeling, it was a fact; something I knew because of hard evidence.

As always, Atip would be ready to add a little to my knowledge.

Saying Goodbye

In our final meeting, Atip surprised me by telling me that he was leaving the Warrior meeting place for good but that, before he left, he wanted to ask me a small favour. Of course, I was more than happy to do anything I could to help and asked him to just let me know what he wanted.

"Before that," he said "let's look at your plan. We know it's a good plan, don't we, because you proved that to yourself by your excellent results? Now, remember that it's very important to capture the names and email addresses of your customers because the hardest part of succeeding is now behind you i.e. finding your customers. Once you have them. Treat them very well, give them more than they expect every time; and they, in turn, will reward you very well indeed.

Now we come to the tweaking. You remember that you did the Planning and the Doing. We now have the results of your project, so you did the Checking. That now leaves the Tweaking. This is something you will *never* finish. Commit yourself to constantly tweaking your approach based upon what works and what does not; and never stop doing this. You will get better and better and achieve ever greater levels of success."

Again, I received excellent advice and was grateful, but the moment was tinged with sadness because I knew he was planning to leave.

"What do you want me to do?" I eventually asked.

"Well," he began "when I joined the meeting place as a Novice, I just couldn't make any money at all."

"Really?"

"Yes. But then a wiser Warrior, kind of, took me under his wing and showed me the ropes and with his guidance, I began to become successful. Eventually, I became what I consider to be a success and one day he told me he was planning to move on."

"Just like you did for me," I said.

"Yes. And he asked me to do something for him before he left. He asked me to help other Novices in the meeting place and to not leave until I had helped to make at least one other person successful. Of course, I agreed. Now, the time has come for me to ask you to do the same thing. Will you agree - you don't have to say yes?"

Of course, I was flabbergasted, but also honoured to think that he thought I was now qualified to help a few others. I had only one question left to ask.

"How do you think I could best do that?"

"You are a writer," he said "use what God has given you."

That was the last time I saw Atip and this book represents my tribute to him, the unsung hero who helped me to finally achieve success.

Reflection

So that's my story ... in the form of a parable.

The book was previously published by White Dove Books (2011) as *The Making of a Warrior,* back when was when I was an active member of the Warrior Forum, hence the warrior reference in the title. It was my first attempt, as a writer, to tackle the medium of *allegory* and, as I enjoyed the writing so much, it has become a style with which I continue to work.

After writing the book, I noticed a discussion at the Warrior Forum about the *meaning* of the text and I found it interesting to note the various interpretations put forth at the time. It is one of the things that interests me most about allegory as a literary form. Clearly, there are a number of very solid business lessons embedded within the *Badass* story, including the importance of developing a strategy and a unique selling proposition (USP). And the inclusion of a slightly *tweaked* version of the *Deming Cycle* (Plan, Do, Check, Tweak) gave me special pleasure.

However, as important as those lessons undoubtedly are, there is a whole lot more to take away from the story, which is why I suggest reading it more than once. Some of the meaning will become more apparent as you begin to take action on your own project, as I most certainly hope you will. In order to get the most out of the book, try to think about each of the following questions in relation to your own situation.

What does Atip mean when he says 'it is only when the student is ready that the teacher can appear?'

What do the archives represent in the allegory?

How many ways are there to make money?

What kind of questions get the best results?

Where do the best answers come from?

Who or what does Lazarus represent in the story?

What did losing the money teach?

How should you start making money?

What is the difference between a product and a service?

What does the presence of competition tell us?

How do we beat the competition?

How do we create an effective plan?

Over the next few pages, I will endeavour to provide my own answers to those questions. But I would really like to encourage you to *stop* reading, at this point, and think about the above questions before reading on.

Study Questions

Q: What does Atip mean when he says 'it is only when the student is ready that the teacher can appear?'

A: It made little sense to me the first time I ever heard the expression, but it is attributed to the Buddha (Siddhartha Guatama Shakyamuni) so you can be sure it is a correct principle. Atip's explanation is that you simply *can't* learn something when you are not ready for the lesson i.e. you might encounter the right information and dismiss it as worthless and yet, the same information on a different day will seem like a revelation. There is no question that this is a fundamental truth.

Q: What do the archives represent in the allegory?

The archives represent the existing *body of knowledge* that is readily available and may be found within every area of human interest. Whatever market you decide to operate within, a wealth of knowledge already exists and is readily available online, often for free, and you should make it your business to thoroughly research your chosen field. Become an expert; find out everything you can before beginning to craft your plan.

Q: How many ways are there to make money?

Atip's initial answer, that there are 'a million ways to make money' was, of course, a figure of speech and his meaning was that there are a *multitude* of ways. But he could not resist joking about the actual number as, when questioned, he revised his number to upwards of a *third of a billion* based on some quick mental arithmetic.

The real point is that wherever there is human need of some sort, there is a corresponding opportunity to be leveraged and such needs are truly manifold.

Q: What kind of questions get the best results?

A: Someone once said that there are no great answers, there are only great questions. But when you ask great questions, you get the best results and, without any doubt whatsoever, the best kind of questions are *not* general in any way; they are very *specific*.

Q: Where do the best answers come from?

You can get *good* answers from those experts who are prepared to share their knowledge with you (like my mentor Atip) and it really can provide a short-cut if you can find people who are experienced in exactly what you are proposing to undertake. But the very best answers come from *within*. When you learn this truth and begin to test it, you will be absolutely astonished at the results. Be specific with the questions that you ask, but 'ask and you shall receive.'

Q: Who or what does Lazarus represent in the story?

A: Beware of those who promise quick and easy success; it has become the hallmark of the scammer. I really enjoyed writing the character of Lazarus into the story. It is not that Lazarus is a scammer, as such, it is more that he is deluded. He represents the message of the scam artist and the folly of quick and easy success without effort. Ruling out luck as a method (as it is completely out of our control) there is always a price to be paid for success and it is measured in terms of sweat; through your own determination and persistence.

Q: What did losing the money teach?

A: On one level, losing the money taught the truth that *if something sounds too good to be true, then it probably is!* But on another level, it taught something more profound. It is a fact that you can know something *intellectually* but it may never affect your behaviour until personal experience proves its true value. If you never have such an experience that connects a specific result with an individual piece of knowledge, then you might never truly learn the lesson. As learning expert David Kolb puts it, "learning is the process whereby knowledge is created through the transformation of experience."

Q: How should you start making money?

A: Atip's answer was that you start by 'not starting' and suggested that you should first concentrate on forming a strategy. Although we have discussed all of the important aspect of strategy, the very first thing he said that you need to do was to identity your *target market*; the specific group of people you intend to serve by offering *products* and *services* designed to help them to overcome their problems.

Q: What is the difference between a product and a service?

A: The answer provided by Searchah26 was that *services* provide an opportunity to benefit from recurring income. If you are looking to do exceptionally well in your own business (as I am sure you are) then you should carefully consider what services you could offer to your target market. Of course, to do this, you must first have thoroughly researched your target market to discover what kind of services they are *already* buying.

Q: What does the presence of competition tell us?

A: Without healthy competition, you should question whether or not the opportunity you are seeking to address really represents a market at all. The presence of competition tells us that there is indeed a *market* i.e. that other people are already making money by providing products and services within that particular space. Although you might think that the presence of the competition is a bad thing, it is completely normal and only to be expected.

Q: How do we beat the competition?

A: The short answer is by developing a winning *strategy*. Your USP should firmly set you apart from the competition. If your product or service has something *desirable* that none of the others (the competition) can provide, this alone *positions* your offering as a natural choice for your prospect. But your *plan* is also a fundamental part of your winning strategy.

Q: So how do we create an effective plan?

A: You must assemble *all* of the above into a concise approach. First, identify your target market and then research it and, in the process, develop a thorough understanding of what characterises that group of people: who they are, what they are trying to achieve and what specific problems they face. Then, develop and package your solution(s) to those problems in the form of products and/or services. Finally, ensure that you get your offerings in front of your target audience by whatever means makes financial sense, whether that is through the medium of advertising, social media, networking, affiliates, word-of-mouth, search engine optimisation or any other reliable method.

Summary

My new business model consists of creating a range of high quality non-fiction books, and then selling them online, without incurring any marketing costs. Creating each book involves putting into practice what we have discussed; finding a market, identifying a suitable problem and producing a viable solution. In my case, getting my books in front of identified target markets involves leveraging the search functions of the online stores; in particular, the Amazon store.

Time will tell whether or not I will manage to reach my financial goal which remains unchanged. But, at the time of writing, I am very optimistic. Now, deep into the execution of my revised business plan, I am already enjoying a good degree of success. Having consistently increased my income every month over the past six month period, it is fair to say that my plan is working.

You may be seeking success right now. Perhaps you are still looking for that little pearl of wisdom that can make the difference and propel you forward toward your goal. Well, I hope you have found something of real value in this little book which was written especially for you. Make sure you read the allegory carefully, again and again if necessary. Annotate the text as the full meaning emerges for you and work on your strategy until you have all of the details worked out.

Remember that you need a Vision, a Plan and a USP (Unique Selling Proposition) that separates you from your competition. Then, once you have developed your strategy, commit yourself to the Plan, Do, Check, Tweak cycle and remember that the checking and tweaking *never* stops. Finally, allow me to wish you well in your own personal journey to success. If you follow the advice above, you will be well on your way.

Part 2 – My New Plan

You may recall that, in the allegory, Atip asked me the question, "After *you* have become successful, will you publish your plan for everyone else to read?" My initial answer to his question was that I was not sure and, because I wanted the business lessons outlined above to be the central message of this work, my original edition of this book did not contain my current plan. But, I realise that my subsequent application of those lessons over the following years might be beneficial to others and so, in that spirit, what now follows are the specifics of my revised business plan.

As a writer, naturally, my plan concerns writing and profiting from my work. Essentially, my approach involves identifying a target market, then creating a book that addresses the challenges faced by that market. With good positioning, my efforts are continually rewarded as I get paid, over and over, day after day, when people find and purchase my information product. Then I repeat that process, incrementally building my income with each iteration of the cycle. That is exactly what I am doing right now and that is the business model I am going to explain to you in the remainder of this book.

With this business model, you don't have to hold stock, you have no employees and no boss. Everything is made from the comfort of your own home (or even Starbucks, if you prefer) your 'info-books' can enable you to do what you want, when you want. Need to increase your income? All you have to do is flip open your laptop and start pounding those keys, create a new informational *non-fiction* book and start selling it. Info-marketing, as I like to call it, gives you the ability to make money from your kitchen table, gain full control over your life and your income. It's certainly the lifestyle for me and, pretty soon, it could be the lifestyle for you too.

It is a wonderful thing that, today, the internet offers the opportunity for us to sell information as a digital download with no physical product to create and nothing to ship. It is an amazing opportunity that simply did not exist for previous generations. In the past, if you wanted to be a writer, you had to work with agents and publishers. They were the gate-keepers that we needed to convince of the marketability of our books. These days, we can just get on with it, publish independently, and test out ideas in real time.

Selling *non-fiction* is a very profitable business, but you need to be in it for the long haul. Don't expect to write one book and knock the ball out of the park. Instead, be content with making each of your books profitable in their own right, generating steady incremental income for you without marketing effort. You will gradually build your income over the course of time because the joy of this business model is that you'll work once and get paid for that work for years to come.

If you focused on nothing more than creating a *catalogue* of non-fiction books, carefully positioned and targeted to provide solutions to problems people face, you would not go far wrong. Of course, that means you have to find problems that people want to solve;

problems for which they are actively seeking-out solutions. It also means you will have to research those problems and come up with good answers. And it means understanding how to position your solution in front of those who are searching.

Your initial investment is your own time, creating the books themselves. You may have some additional costs in editing and cover design, though it is certainly true that you can do these things yourself. That said, covers are especially important and it is often worth paying for a decent cover if your design skills are not yet up to muster. It is a skill you can definitely learn - I know because I create almost all of my own covers. I was not very good at the start, but my current covers are as good as anyone else's within my chosen genres.

What You Have To Do

Creating a good quality, in-demand book is your first step. The business model is simple. It's so simple most newbies think there must be more to it, so they keep looking for something more complicated. They stumble upon the truth, then get up as though nothing had ever happened and carry on looking for something more complicated.

Here's what you do:

- Start by finding a suitable problem

- Search marketplaces for existing solutions

- Estimate your chances of ranking (in Amazon and other stores) for a relevant keyword/phrase(s)

- If you don't stand a chance of ranking well, go back and find another problem

- Create a book that offers the solution to the specific problem you selected

- Get it in front of your target market

- Find another suitable problem and repeat the above procedure

Okay, so let's go through the process in some detail. Firstly, there is the matter of finding a specific problem with which you will work. At first this may seem difficult, but as you progress, you will come to realise that suitable problems are all around you and your friends, family, associates and so on – everywhere there are people, there are problems too.

As an example, let me tell you that whenever I face a personal problem that I have to research, solve or gain access to the solution, especially if it's a difficult nut to crack, I ask myself: *is there a book in this*? Over the years, I have faced a number of minor medical problems and I have written books for each of them. They did not *all* do well – that is because, not all problems were suitable and I did not know that at the start.

But some of those books, have sold consistently, over a period of many years and because of the way the Amazon algorithm works (more about that later) they have gained greater traction over time. This means that they actually sell, without *any* marketing effort at all! But getting to this point requires that we can at least rank somewhere meaningfully, in the first few pages of Amazon for a relevant keyword search.

In order for us to rank well for a keyword search, we first need to find problems with certain characteristics:

Suitable Problems

 - Steady search volume

 - Relatively few competing books available

 - Existing books poorly targeted

There is absolutely no point, as far as we are concerned, in writing a book that solves a problem that nobody cares about. So you need to be able to assess search volume for the bookstore(s) you will be using to position your books. There are many tools available on the market, both free and paid and I have included a handy resource section for you that lists some excellent free tools, at the end.

What we are looking for is <u>steady</u> search volume not necessarily high search volume. If you can find a problem that gets a few thousand searches per month (or even just a few hundred) and your book is on the first page of the Amazon search results, you can soon have a steady flow of income trickling into your bank account.

Sometimes, this is remarkably easy because, quite simply, you may find a problem for which there are relatively few books available. One of my health books fell into this category and is now not only on page #1 of the Amazon results, but is the <u>number one</u> result for its targeted phrase. So I can tell you from experience that this is still possible even in this day and age when the search results seem to be saturated. It is the main reason you should be concentrating on *non-fiction* if you are concerned with generating profit.

One of the reasons you can still have the edge over your competitors is that other people do not understand, very well, how the ranking algorithms work for the various ebook stores. So they end up not doing their keyword research properly, or they do not choose their titles well enough. As a consequence, their books end up being poorly targeted.

One you have identified a problem that has steady search volume i.e. we know people are searching for solutions, the next step is to look at the competition. These are books that are already well-placed in the major ebook stores. A side note here: bear in mind that Amazon is *not* the only show in town. There are (currently) five stores that are worthy of your time and attention.

The Big Five

- Amazon

- Apple iBooks

- Barnes & Noble

- Kobo

- Google Play

Although we are going to focus on Amazon, as the largest bookseller in the world, you should always bear in mind that if you can't make it on Amazon, you may well be able to make it on another store. The reason is very straightforward: they all use *different* ranking algorithms. A well-optimised title and description can end up doing very well on certain stores, even if it effectively 'bombs' on Amazon. So, make sure you experiment with all of those five stores.

Go to <u>each</u> of the above stores and put yourself into the shoes of a potential customer. What would such a person be typing into the search box if they were looking for a solution to the problem you have identified? Type in some queries that occur to you. Use the <u>same</u> queries in each of those five stores and compare the first few pages of results. Notice the differences in the listings. Yes, it is true that not every author will have published on each of those platforms (just the smart ones) but even for those that have, a short time comparing and contrasting the search results will help you to understand that different <u>algorithms</u> produce different results.

While you are researching the competition, you are trying to answer the question: can I get my book into the first few pages of the results for a particular keyword phrase? You can definitely do that if the number of books returned for the phrase is relatively few. That is exactly what happened for one of the health books I mentioned above. But you can **also** do it, at least, on some of those sites, even when there is a fair amount of competition. The reason is simple: it is because many of your competitor's listings will be poorly optimised – basically, a lot of people just don't understand what they are doing in this respect!

Poorly Optimised Listings

- Keyword phrase *not* in title or subtitle

- Keyword phrase *not* in keyword fields

- Keyword phrase *not* in description

In order to examine the keyword fields of competing books, you will need to use a tool that is capable of scraping the data from Amazon. But the other aspects of the listing are right there in front of your eyes. You can quite easily see whether or not your competitor has used the keyword phrase in those places. If the keyword phrase does not appear in all of those fields, you can definitely do a better job of optimisation than your competitors – and, if you do that, your listing *will* appear in the search results for those sites that use algorithms which are more focussed on <u>relevance</u>.

Algorithms

Yes, it is time to talk in some detail about algorithms; what they are, how they work and how they are relevant to us as writers. Hopefully, you have already taken on board the truth that different ebook stores use different search algorithms. This is exactly why you can be successful at one site, whilst you are unsuccessful at another.

Hopefully, this should resolve the question of whether you should distribute 'wide' or accept Amazon's exclusivity terms and put your book into the *Kindle Unlimited* program. If you were going to write fiction, then it is a different matter – some genres (particularly romance) can do very well in *Kindle Unlimited*. But we are talking about non-fiction and there is no question about it, you need to distribute your books *wide* i.e. to the big five stores listed above or, at least, experiment with doing so – you know, *check* and *tweak* based on your own results!

Now, firstly, let's consider the question: what is an algorithm? Quite simply, it is a set of rules. In our case, we are interested in the search algorithms of the ebook stores i.e. the rules they use to put books in order following a keyword or key-phrase search. Amazon quite helpfully tells us their rules and they are known as the *A9 Algorithm*.

The A9 Algorithm

The Amazon algorithm uses the following factors to determine the order that books are placed in, following a keyword phrase search. To get the Amazon *algo* working for you, you should ensure your books conform to the following recommendations:

- Priced to turn better profit than the competition

- Description includes your keywords

- Keyword in the title and/or subtitle

- Consistency of sales (sales volume)

- Clicks on your listing (conversion)

- Quality of cover

- Spelling, grammar, editing and quality

- Number of verified reviews

You should pay attention to *all* of the above factors in the creation of your book listings. But if there is one thing, above all else that you need to grasp that will help you to understand how and why Amazon ranks books in the order it does, it is the following.

The MAMM Factor is King

All of the above factors conspire to do one thing and one thing only. It is to *make Amazon the most money* (MAMM)!

Total Revenue = Number of Books Sold x Sales Price

Optimising your listing for your *keyword phrase* gets you into the listings that are returned after a search.

Unless you deliberately optimise your book listing by getting the targeted keyword phrase into *all* the right places (see above) you will **not** be in the running at all. So this is *very* important - understand that you will never rank for a keyword phrase for which you have not optimised!

But there is more to it than that. After you publish, *every 24 hours thereafter*, Amazon will look at the amount of money (total revenue) that your book has made in relation to the other books in the search results for *each keyword result* your book is placed within. If your book consistently makes more money than the one above, your book will get moved up the listings. If your book consistently makes less money than the one below, your book gets moved down.

So, you see, it is a two phase process.

Phase 1 – get your book into the first few pages of the search results for a keyword phrase search that has some volume behind it. You need to be in it to win it!

Phase 2 – do **everything** you can to make more money for Amazon and watch your book gradually climb the listings.

People never talk about the second part of this process because it is poorly understood within author and book marketing circles, but it **is** how Amazon works! And it is why you **can** succeed because, provided you can get indexed by Amazon for a keyword search, your book will gradually move up the listings if you pay attention to the other factors (see above) that can get your book selling better than the competition.

An understanding of this process will also help you to see why, if you want to make money on Amazon, you have a better chance with *non-fiction* than with fiction. Writers of fiction have relatively few keyword phrases for which they can optimise, and some of the most desirable are even disallowed by Amazon. So fiction books, unless they can gain sales somehow will sink like a stone in the Amazon store, very quickly.

That is why fiction writers have become so obsessed with product launches. They pay for promotions such as *Bookbub* or *AMS* ads (Amazon Marketing Services) in the hope of generating enough of an initial spike in sales to take advantage of the MAMM factor (make Amazon more money). They hope that, as a result, they will bag a decent slot in the organic search results and 'also bought' slots. But in the current climate, even if they achieve that aim, unless their short term visibility leads to a steady stream of organic sales, they are destined to be consigned to failure.

Even fiction writers who do well in the short term can become history in a very short time if they lose their ability to generate sales. Our non-fiction books on the other hand, *at worst*, will sink to the bottom of our targeted keyword results – if you have chosen well, you'll still be in the first few pages for your keyword phrase, so you are still findable! However, if you have paid proper attention to the other factors listed above, your book will gradually <u>rise</u> in the results for your keyword phrase, without ***any*** marketing effort whatsoever!

Read the above section again and let it sink in – an understanding of the *A9 Algorithm* is absolutely vital for achieving long term success on Amazon.

Finding a Market

If you can identify a specific group of people that are trying to achieve something, they may have a whole host of problems for you to help them with. In this situation you have found not just an opportunity, but a **market** and you can continue to write for that market, building your reputation over time as you offer viable solutions for the various problems they face. In doing so, it is very important that you understand this simple truth: create books your target market is <u>already</u> demanding.

You have to create books that address your market's problems and, sometimes, those problems will be silly things because your market doesn't really understand the problem they have. When you're creating non-fiction books, the first step is learning to listen to your target market and only then begin to create the books <u>they</u> want and need. This is a mistake I made with my very first book. I created it first and then started trying to sell it – believe me, this is entirely the wrong way round.

You can hang out in relevant online forums to find out how your target market thinks, what problems they are experiencing and what they are looking for. You need to identify a specific, *difficult-to-solve* problem and then go and find out the answer and give it to them in the form of your book. You will make *far* more sales in the long run if you get this right. Learn to listen and understand your market and understand their pains and frustrations *first*; create the book *second*. Creating the book should be relatively easy once you have done your research (since you're simply answering real questions you will have identified at the forums) and selling it should be a fairly straightforward too, because your target group will be already actively looking for what you will create.

A Vital First Step

If you've never made a dime online, you need to take this away: learn the basics and then make sure you get really good at one thing in particular. FOCUS – **F**ollow **O**ne **C**ourse **U**ntil **S**uccessful. That is exactly what I did; I never gave up on my main project. I worked at it *until* I became successful and it took me seven years of hard work to do it. Hopefully, it will take you a lot less with my guidance.

Profitable niches are all around you.

It's better still when the niche has repeat buyers. It's why *health*, *wealth* and *relationships* are the three BIG markets that are so attractive for targeting non-fiction books. We all need money, we all need to look after our health (and will have health problems) and we all want to have long-term, fulfilling relationships with a loving partner. If you're not sure where to start then pick one of these three big, proven markets. Within each market there are lots of *niches* for you to target, profit from and expand into.

What Are You Passionate About?

There are two schools of thought on making money with your passion. One schools says it's a great way to start because you're doing what you love which means you're more likely to stick with it and see it through to the end - I couldn't agree more. The other school says go where the money is because passions aren't profitable. This is *only* good advice if you can really stick with whatever niche you decide upon.

In the past, I have been involved in niches that I didn't care about. In fact, some of them bored me to tears and I consequently ended up with some finished projects and a few that remain unfinished to this day. A lot of people choose to start writing and marketing books because they hate their day job; they hate the daily commute, hate their boss or don't earn enough money. Make sure you don't end up replacing your day job with something else you don't like doing; there's absolutely no reason to do so.

Existing Skills & Expertise

Learning to leverage your skills and knowledge is a fundamental skill as an author and marketer and it can help you find success much, much faster. If your passion is profitable, then follow it wholeheartedly. If your passion isn't profitable, then start by making a list of what you're good at. This list might consist of skills you use at work, at home, in your leisure time, or something you did at some time in the past.

The quickest way to enter a market and build your business is through leverage and the quickest way for you to get started is by asking yourself "what skills do I already have?" What problems have you experienced first-hand and could offer good quality advice on? Don't be scared to think outside the box and don't exclude life-skills.

The other day I was flicking through old cover issues of parenting magazines for ideas and kept coming across two subjects.

- Dealing with temper tantrums

- Helping fussy eaters

Two life skills I'm sure many mothers and fathers have first-hand experience at, and have managed to deal with. And even if you're not a parent or your children were delightful, I'm sure you could very easily research either topic and create a report very quickly.

If you find yourself doubting yourself or questioning whether or not you're qualified to provide the required solution, you're not alone. Remember expertise is relative. On a scale of 1 to 10, if you're a level 5 then market your book to people at level 1 – 4. It's no different to the science teacher at primary school, high school or university. They're all qualified to teach at different levels and you should think in exactly the same way.

Is Your Niche Profitable?

Now, I can't give you a formula for determining how much profit there is to be made from a particular niche. But you can stack the odds of success in your favour by running through some key factors before you think about creating your book. Make sure you can answer the majority of the following questions with a *yes*, before you start researching and writing.

Once you identify a niche, think about keyword phrases that people might type into Amazon. Then go to Google – yes Google – and type-in a keyword phrase. Take note of the absence or presence of sponsored advertising in the SERPS (search engine results pages). If people are paying for advertising (those are the *sponsored ads* that you find down the right hand side and also at the top of the search results in Google) that is a sure sign there is money to be made. Do this over a period of time because nobody is going to continue to pay for advertising if they are losing money.

Also note whether or not there magazines devoted to the niche subject you have identified. As we might appreciate, magazines are only produced if the market is passionate and there is money to be made. Not only does the presence of magazines demonstrate that your niche is alive, well and spending money, magazines are also a great source for niche market research.

If there are already competing and related books in the Amazon search results, it's generally a good sign. If you're creating a non-fiction book, there *should* be competing offerings. But the availability of such books does not indicate that the market is actually *buying*. The truth is that lots of people are not making *any* money at all. But you can quite easily figure out if a book is selling by looking at its Amazon BSR (best seller rank). This is a number that is shown at the foot of a book's listing.

If the Amazon BSR figure is not shown at all for a particular book, it means that it has *not* sold a single copy! If the figure is in the millions, the book is not selling well. But, if the rank is consistently in the thousands, you have found something that is selling. The following table will give you some idea of how many daily sales a book is actually getting

Amazon BSR and Sales

BSR	Daily Sales (Avg)
200,000	1
100,000	2
50,000	5
25,000	10
10,000	26
5,000	50

Treat the above as a rough guide. It is accurate at the time of writing, but the relationship between the numbers will naturally change over the course of time, as more books get added to the Amazon store and the behaviour of buyers changes too. However, there are various tools that can provide you with accurate, up-to-date data – please see the resource list for details.

Checking my own books as of *today*, I have one particular book ranked at **#559,455**. It is a business book, available both as a paperback and a Kindle book. Although, it is selling just less than 1 book per day on average, I have it priced at $9.99 (the maximum you can charge on Amazon and still retain a 70% royalty) and over the last 30 days, it has earned the following:

eBook	Paperback
28.86	41.85

That's **$62.71** (USD) for just one non-fiction book and that's just the *dot-com* site i.e. the US store. The other stores (mainly those in Europe and India) all bring in additional income; last month I actually sold 56 copies of that book in India alone.

At present, I have 22 non-fiction books and 4 fiction books in my current catalogue. Because my method requires my books to gain traction and generate sales without marketing effort, my fiction books rarely, if ever, sell any copies at all; just an odd one every now and then. But my *non-fiction* all adds up to bring in a consistent income and I am constantly working at adding new books to my catalogue all the time.

The hardest part is making your *first* book and getting your *first* buyers. It's also the most expensive part in terms of time and money. But your second book allows you to leverage those assets. After your first book you'll know your market much better. You'll have feedback from your buyers, and it's much easier to create a new book in the same market than to create a new book for a different market. That's why, ideally, you want a market that allows you to create multiple books that can all be sold to the same people.

Niche Selection Action Step

Make a list of ten different niches you're drawn toward. Don't fuss, don't sweat, just pick ten that catch your eye and/or interest you, and get ready to do a little profitability check on them by applying the above questions. If your niche turns out to be a winner, great; if it's not what you'd hoped for, don't worry, move on to the next. Most non-fiction authors operate in a number of different niches and quite often the niche you start out in isn't the one you'll finish up in. Life has a funny way of taking us to places we'd never imagined.

Use the above checks to test each of the niches you have identified. Now, from that analysis, make a shortlist of just three niches that are both profitable and appealing to you. Finally, from that shortlist, pick <u>one</u> of them to concentrate on - the other two can sit on the back-burner for now, as projects that can be picked up some time in the future. This process may be time consuming, but it is absolutely crucial to your success and, if you follow these steps, you should soon be able to identify the <u>right</u> target niche for your first non-fiction book.

Quick Tip: You can shortcut the above process by making use of research tools. There are a few tools that I personally use for market research and they deliver excellent results. See my resource list (at the end) for more details.

Researching Your Book

It's time to roll up your sleeves and start researching your chosen niche market for the purpose outlining your content. But before going any further, remember that it's very easy to get caught up in research, make endless pages of notes and then get distracted and consequently, end up putting your project to one side - don't let that happen! Keep an eye on your time and be disciplined. It's better to have to go back and get more information than it is to do hours and hours of research, end up with material you never need and get bogged down or overwhelmed.

Your first task is to get enough information to get a first draft together and see what your book looks like from there. You're going to start with a process of accumulation. Accumulating information and compartmentalising it as you see fit. Don't get hung up on the detail right now. Just collect relevant and useful information, put it where you think it should go and get your book underway. You can always change it, move it and amend things later.

As you are researching information you will recognise themes and these will become your chapters. Just copy and paste the information you find into a *Word Document* to keep it organized or simply *bookmark* the sites for future reference using your internet browser. By the way, I hardly feel it necessary to include the following because I am sure you would never think of doing so, but **don't** plagiarise other people's content. The information you collect from various sources is for reference purposes and idea generation, but your book should be your own original content.

Hop over to Google and type in <u>any</u> question that relates to your chosen niche. Scroll through the results and find forums, message boards, blogs and social interaction sites such as *Yahoo Answers* where real people are meeting online and asking for help. If you don't find anything first time, don't forget to use Google's 'discussion' and 'blogs' settings to narrow down your search results. Forums and discussion boards are great because people will share their innermost secrets online, even with strangers, simply because there is no embarrassment online. You can hide behind a computer screen, use a fake name, fake location and effectively become anyone you want to be.

- Copy and paste questions that people are asking

- Copy and paste helpful replies

It's important that you copy and paste simply because you'll gradually learn the language, including any specialist terms that people in your target niche are using. This is important when you write your sales copy (blurb) because you want to mentally connect with future buyers and build rapport to gain trust.

As you study the replies to questions, try to remain impartial to the advice offered. Some advice will be good but there will be a lot of 'misinformed' individuals out there. Take note, because this is a great way to find a combination of real world information gleaned from experience as well as the myths that are circulating too.

Real world conversations are happening on Twitter and Facebook. So find businesses engaged in building relationships through Facebook and Twitter, then listen-in to see what people are saying. You'll find random tips, trails to good sources of information, myths and – again – you listen-in to real world conversations. What people are saying, the problems they're having and the exact words they use to describe those problems.

Be sensible when you do your research, don't take everyone's advice as expert and remember, in most instances (this goes for newspapers and television reports too), the information you read is often only someone else's opinion. Blogs, forums and message boards definitely have their fair share of experts, people who've been around years and are often more than qualified to give advice. Find those forum experts – the one's that others respect – and read their posts, their replies and their opinions. That way you can soon find out what's right, what's wrong and what's misunderstood.

Find established websites offering information and services. You can find a wealth of information on the websites of companies who are using information to educate and build trust with new clients. This is especially useful for the health niche where research papers and medical journals are often referenced. Websites providing real reviews on books in your niche are another great source of information.

If you've decided to pick a niche in which you are already an expert or that you are passionate about, then there's a good chance you have a stack of books on it already. If you don't have books on the topic just ask some friends, buy them or go visit the library. As I glance over at my bookshelf I see row upon row of books on business and money matters.

So, right now you've got pretty much everything you need to make a book. You've got forum posts with questions and advice, some will be good and some will be really bad. Remember that the bad advice is *great* because it provides a chance to debunk some popular myths. Now it is time to generate your *outline* – your overall plan for the book.

Remember the good old garden peas! PPPPPPP ... **P**roper **P**lanning and **P**reparation **P**revents **P**articularly **P**oor **P**erformance. You might know a slightly different version ;)

Mind Mapping is my preferred method for **planning** a book because it's very easy to get a top-down overview of your project. You are able to clearly see everything on one page and so it's easy to get the flow of ideas right. The nice thing about Mind Mapping is the ability to see everything and move information about easily. You might start with something in chapter one and later decide to move it to chapter four.

At this stage, I personally like to work with pen and paper. I make a Mind Map by starting in the middle of the page by drawing a circle. In the circle, I put my working title, then I draw radial lines which each represent a chapter. Looking at the information gathered in the previous steps, online, I discern areas of interest that become the themes around which my chapters are based. I give each of the radial lines a title (these are my chapter headings) then I split each line into sub-divisions with topics distilled from my research.

There are other methods of outlining, but this is how I actually work. You might prefer a different way of working – that's okay – the important thing is to get an outline together that has all of your individual topics organised into chapters in the best possible order. You are then ready to move on to the actual legwork of writing. The hard bit is having the discipline to sit down, compile and create the book. This may be where you have to remind yourself about the money, the lifestyle and the holidays you'll eventually be having in the sun.

Creating Your Book

While it might not feel like it, when you've complied your research much of the hard work is actually done. All that's left now is to organize your information and write out your notes. This is also the step where many people end up with a half-finished book. Stick a picture on the wall or put a post-it note on your computer reminding you WHY you're creating this book - the time, the money, the lifestyle or simply because you hate your job.

If you find yourself thinking negatively, kick those thoughts right out of your head; they won't help you and they will just get in the way of you completing the project. As you write out your notes, remember to think of this as your first draft. Don't fuss and don't worry about editing as you go. That will only slow you down. Instead get into the groove and just start writing.

Here are a few different types of book you might like to consider writing. They are great for non-fiction and relatively easy to write too, because they each have a distinctive sequential format.

List Books

Many lists you can find online, like *The Worlds 50 Richest People* can make great book ideas in themselves. Some niches lend themselves well to this, for example, *The Top 100 Traffic Methods Online* or *10 Ways to Lose a Pound of Fat a Day*. There are various ways you could organise such a *list book*. You could list the methods randomly or you could start with the easiest and finish with the hardest. As you want to motivate your readers to keep reading, you could start strong with your best methods, then add in the less popular methods and then you finish strong so your readers go away "pumped" and ready to take action.

If you look after children, work from home and have to stop and start frequently then List Books are really good to try first because they're much easier to put down and subsequently pick up where you left off.

Step-by-Step Guides

Many information books fall into this category and it's the one we'll focus on for the most part. How to build websites, chicken coops, raised flower beds, garages, sheds or learning how to pack on extra muscle; all of these ideas would lend themselves very well to the *step-by-step* approach. Step-by-step books are simple guides that you follow in a logical order and the secret is to make that sequence as clear as possible. Spell out what action the person needs to take after each section or chapter.

Q & A Books

Imagine a gardening book for beginners who would like to grow their own vegetables. You ask the keen gardeners you know, you check forums and collect the most commonly asked questions and problems. You ask gardeners what their top tips for new vegetable growers would be, what mistakes they made and what they would do if they were to start from scratch. Then create a book where you type each question and answer it.

A-Z Books

The A-Z of Gardening sits on my bookshelf and the content simply runs through various techniques in alphabetical order. That is an example of an A-Z Book. A cook book where *A* contains all the recipes whose key ingredients such as Aubergine, Apples and Almonds might provide another example. Baby names, dog breeds or perhaps the *A-Z Guide to a Richer Life*. As you can see, it is a special category of List Book that essentially makes finding something a whole lot easier - there's not much more to say.

Time to Start Writing

The type of book you create will largely be determined by your niche and the type of information you have collected. But, do at least consider the above formats. The great thing about both list books and alphabetical books is you can just get on with writing them; each section is a small chunk and you know exactly what is going into that chunk (all the stuff beginning with the letter *A* will go into the *A chapter* etc).

When it comes to creating a step-by-step guide you can think of each chapter as a miniature version of your entire book dealing with a specific topic. Each chapter will go through the points – step-by-step – and in the most logical order. It definitely helps to have a structure for each chapter that you can stick to throughout the book.

Here's a basic outline for a *step-by-step* book.

Step 1 – What's in it for me?

As nice as it would be, not many people will get on with something until they know what's in it for them. Your reader might be motivated by money, power, relationships or making a contribution to others that makes them feel good. Or maybe they're really lazy and just want reassurance they can do this.

So it can be very helpful to start your book and each subsequent chapter by explaining *why* they should do what they're about to read. It's good for you too because if they understand *why* they'll feel much more motivated and be more likely to use and apply your information. That's good for testimonials, future sales and your karma.

Step 2 – Quick overview of the subject

Instead of going in cold, give your readers a quick overview of what they're about to learn. You don't have to go into a lot of detail, just give them a bird's eye view of what is ahead of them.

It's a good idea to whet their appetite and make them a little curious so they will want to find out more. You can remind them again about the end result to keep them motivated and on track. Plus it will help to give them a skeleton of your ideas that they can flesh out as they work through your book and deepen their understanding.

Step 3 – Your Step-by-Step Book Structure

In the same way that you have organized your chapters in a sequential order, organize the information within each chapter into a logical order that flows. To start with, you simply need to cut and paste; move your information around and get ready to start writing it out in your own words.

Remember to always keep your target market in mind. If they're beginners remember to break everything down into minute detail and don't worry about it being too simple. If your audience already understands the essence of a section, then they can skim-read the parts they don't know. It's better to be thorough than it is to assume your reader already knows everything. Make zero assumptions and break everything into the most basic elements so everyone can understand. No one will ever complain your book is 'too clear' or 'too easy to understand'.

Step 4 – Add Stories, Examples, Quotes or Pictures

If you've ever read a sales letter and got sucked in, there's a good chance it's because of a compelling story. One of the most common stories on sales letters in the Internet Marketing niche is "*I was broke, now I'm not – If I can do it, you can too.*" Do you recognise it?

Stories are so powerful because we humans love them, we seem to be programmed to be able to remember them too. History was passed on this way before writing. Stories create pictures in our minds and we're simply wired to tune in. When you come across stories, case studies examples or quotes in your research, make sure you use them in your books. They can add a lot of value to your content if they make understanding the subject easier or help to put the information into context (last time I'll mention it – don't plagiarise i.e. use your own words).

Stories break-up your text, make it more enjoyable to read and more memorable too. If people enjoy your books then they're more likely to talk about them, recommend them and buy future books you create.

Step 5 – Summarize and help with the tough parts

One of the best bits of advice I ever read for article writing was as simple as this:

- Tell them what you're going to tell them (the introduction)

- Tell them what you want to tell them (the body)

- Tell them what you just told them (the conclusion)

A summary at the end of your chapter is the perfect place to put everything together, round it all off and tie everything up as a neat little package. We don't have the best of memories, so it's also a great place to remind people of the most important points and what to do next. If you know your market and you know their pains and frustration there's a good chance you also know exactly where they're going to stumble. You can finish your chapters by picking some of the biggest stumbling blocks they're likely to encounter and reveal what they need to do to overcome those hurdles.

Writer's Block

"Write fearlessly, edit ruthlessly"- Source Unknown

As you sit down to write, your mind may well go blank. You might sit there wondering where to start and what to do. Relax, don't worry just open up your word processor and get ready. Legendary copywriter, Eugene Schwartz, set a timer for 33 minutes and 33 seconds and then just sat there with nothing, other than a screen in front of him, until his mind got so bored it would simply start to work.

Start to "*write fearlessly*" it doesn't have to be perfect, it doesn't have to be grammatically correct. Just write based on the notes you've made for that chapter. Don't think too much (you're only tidying up the notes you've already written out) and just start typing. Minimize the amount of time thinking "what next?" by sticking to your step-by-step book *structure*. Open your Word Document up, start writing and explaining why they need to take this course of action, then run through the step-by-step guide and finish up with a summary and overcome the stumbling blocks they'll likely encounter.

Stick to a plan, a routine and a system that eliminates thinking time and lets you get on with taking action.

Proof Reading

When your first draft is completed, leave it alone for a period of about one week and then come back and read through it from the beginning, editing as you go. This gap between creation and editing is absolutely *essential* if you are to spot your own typos. Unless you can read your book as if it is someone else's work, your brain will move characters into the correct sequence without your conscious knowledge and thereby make editing and correcting very difficult, if not impossible.

Michael Masterson wrote a book called *Ready, Fire, Aim – Zero to $100 Million in No Time Flat*. It's a good book and well worth reading. Essentially, he says that the majority of us see an opportunity, get ready, aim, aim some more, keep aiming and by the time we're ready to take action the opportunity (or enthusiasm) has been and gone. It's definitely true that many people spend too much time thinking, contemplating and then failing to hit the target or even pull the trigger. To some extent, we all need to think *Ready, Fire, Aim* in other words, get it done, and get it out there - but <u>not</u> at the expense of editing!

You owe it to your readers to have, at very least one, and preferably two proof-reading sessions for the entire text of your completed manuscript. The book you are now reading was subjected to three proof-edits and, although there were very few typos spotted in the third pass, there were still a few corrections to be made.

When proof-reading, if you come across extra words and sentences that don't make sense, or blocks of text that are just too big – edit them and be *ruthless* with your editing. If you've really been writing fearlessly then there's a very good chance you've got too many unnecessary words such as *this, that, like, if, but, what, when* and other filling words that basically do nothing.

Cut them out and make your sentences short, active and punchy. Keep your paragraphs short and relevant. Long sentences, long paragraphs and big blocks of writing can put people off. And, of course, use your computer's spell checker and grammar checker to help iron out the creases.

Accept that you may never be 100% happy with your book. You will always want to change it but neither of those facts will stop it from selling. The other day, I read about a guy who had finally finished his first book after a year working on it. A year! It's probably nearly perfect and I really hope it's good too because if his first book – his market test – fails then that's a whole year down the drain. After you have sold *your* book, have received feedback and you are confident it's worth the extra time and effort, you can consider improving it further.

A simple alternative to proof-reading your own text is to get someone to do it for you. Just ask your partner or a close friend. They don't need to be an expert and, in many cases, it can be ideal if they are not. You are *not* looking for ideas; just for good English and logical information flow. If they point out something to you that they don't like, don't defend your position; just thank that person. You might think of giving them something in return for doing this important work on your behalf.

Proof Reading Action Step

With your first book, you should be trying to build a loyal fan base that will enjoy your information so much they will want to buy from you again in the future. The very minimum you owe them is to spell check and read through your book at least once, preferably two or three times. But remember to leave your book at least <u>one week</u> each time, before going back to edit it. Believe me, this method not only works, I believe it is absolutely essential if you are going to proof your own work.

Read your work out loud and clearly – it's amazing how you can read sentences in your head just fine but they sound cumbersome and awkward when reading them aloud. When you edit, don't start to re-write your book - good enough is good enough - and big changes can wait for the next version. You may well think of extra information, as you go, and be tempted to go off on tangents as you edit your work. But be disciplined: have a notepad to hand and jot these ideas down. They can be included in updates to your work or even give you ideas for brand new books to sell in the future.

Formatting Your Book

The most important thing about your book is that you want people to find it easy and enjoyable to read. Keep your documents clear and clean – focus on content over style. One of the reasons *Thesis* is such a popular Wordpress Theme is because it allows you to present your content very clearly. If your eye is not being drawn to the text then it's being drawn elsewhere. Your book is exactly the same. One big factor here is the fonts you employ and the way you layout your book. Strangely enough it's a component your readers are unlikely to notice. What I mean is they may find it hard to read something or notice their eyes are getting tired and not realize it's because the font used was not designed for a specific purpose like headlines, sign-writing or novelty.

Personally, for eBook body text, I prefer Times New Roman 12 point - the typeface used in this book - an 18 point sans face for headings and 14 point for subheads. It's never a good idea to go 'over the top' with different font styles. Three is the 'magic number'. You can use one font for headlines, one for sub-heads and one for the main body of your text. If you use more fonts, it starts to interfere with readability.

One time, I remember listening to a story by Terry Dean who would always open his seminars and books with his personal story of how he went from pizza delivery driver to successful marketer. One day he stopped telling his story and his income started to drop. You can be sure that he soon went back to his tried and tested formula for his introduction. Remember that you might have buyers who already know who you are, but you'll also have people who don't know who you are, who need to be inspired and need to know why they should listen to you. Opening with your story is a great way to bolster business, connect with your market and brand yourself. If you're going to use an author introduction consider adding a photo too (it'll help your market remember you and put a face to a name when you contact them again in the future).

A nice way to add appeal to your book is by using text-boxes, indents and quotes. These make elements of your text stand out from the main body of your book. I've used a few within these chapters, in addition to some short lists and bullet points, to make information a little easier to read, break up the text and hopefully make it easier on the eye. If you don't already know how to use the *table of contents* generation feature that is built-in to your word processor, then take a few minutes to learn because it can save you endless hours.

It might sound obvious to include a table of contents but I've seen many an eBook and even real books that do not include a proper table of contents. Ultimately it's down to you, but I strongly recommend you provide one so your users can quickly skim through your information and subsequently find things quickly. Not only does it help them build a mental picture of what's coming up in the chapters ahead it's also useful for speed readers who can digest the information faster. With a little bit of imagination you can give your chapters interesting names (or write them like a *"How to..."* bullet point). This is a great way to increase curiosity and encourage your buyers to actually read and enjoy your information.

Your cover is a very important part of the book creation process. Done well, a good cover increases the perceived value of your book and can make a downloadable book look like a million dollars though it is actually just a bunch of electrons saved on your computer - it's not even a physical book at all. That said, it is quite easy to create a paperback these days as it is an option within the KDP platform. If you have decent design skills, there is no reason you should not create your own covers. But – really – this is where you have to be super-critical of your own work. Your cover has to stack-up against the professionally designed covers in your genre. So make you are honest with yourself. If your own cover does not cut the mustard, get someone with the necessary skills to create one for you. It need not be an expensive option.

Finally, if someone buys your book and they're happy with it, then you've become a trusted source of information. So remember to promote your other works (when you have them available) within the content of your book. Finish your book with an 'about the author' section where you list your other titles and provide links to other related books. There are various ways to do this effectively – see the resource section for some excellent tools.

How to Create Your Book

If you are going to publish only on Kindle, then you can simply upload a Word document and your cover and the KDP platform will do all the necessary conversion for you. However, other stores and distributors will require alternative formats, with EPUB format being something of a standard these days and by far the most common option.

If you are planning to publish your bool *wide* i.e. to multiple stores, the EPUB option is the best format to work with, so get a copy of the free ebook creation software *Calibre* (see resource list) and learn how to use it. It will save you a lot of time and effort because once you can format and create your book as an EPUB, you can distribute it anywhere. In addition to Word documents, even KDP accept EPUBs. You might consider using an aggregator site such as *Smashwords* or

Draft2Digital to distribute your books to a wide range of stores. If you decide to use *Smashwords* for this purpose (as I do) do not be tempted get into their preferred method of uploading Word files into what they call the *Meat Grinder*. Instead, simply upload your EPUB. It all works just fine and, believe me, it can save you hours and hours of headache.

Your Blurb

When you break it down to the nuts and bolts of making a sale you have to remember that your visitors don't know you and they don't know anything about your book. Somehow, they have found your book listing, which is great, but now they find you asking for their money. You need to overcome these barriers - these objections - and help them to feel comfortable with buying your book. Your 'blurb' is the text you'll be using to convince your visitors to buy. It's all about getting the best conversion rate possible i.e. converting visitors to buyers.

A good blurb should multiply and maximize the number of sales you make. Many people make the mistake of thinking that the art of copywriting does not apply to a book blurb, but they could not be more wrong – at least when it comes to non-fiction blurbs. Copywriters are the guys who write the letters about credit cards for your bank, they work for pharmaceutical companies, politicians, investment banks, holiday brochures, newsletters and so on.

A good copywriter can significantly improve the conversion rate of your blurb. Copywriters have to do much more than just 'write' copy, they need to understand the powers of persuasion, how to push emotional hot buttons and position books and brands. Start hanging out on copywriting forums and listen-in and you will learn some of the best copywriting and marketing tips you can find online.

Writing the Blurb Yourself

The job of your blurb is to get your book converting and turning a profit. If your book proves to be a smash hit with greater potential you may decide to invest in professional editing, cover design and blurb writing to really ramp things up. However, at least at first, you will probably wish to write your own blurbs. This section should help you with the basics of getting into the copywriter's mind-set and help you write better blurbs that convert visitors into book sales.

Remember – it's all about your market and what's in it for them. You should already know your market, their pains and frustrations, the words they use and the solutions they're looking for. You did a lot of the hard work when you researched your book and since you've hopefully written it to answer those questions, writing your blurb should be a lot easier.

Because you chose a market with competition, you can read the blurbs of rival books. This is a great shortcut for finding the hottest emotional triggers, the biggest questions and the value that other books are offering – then you can do it better. As you browse the blurbs of best-selling books, you may start to notice some similarities and trends. The headlines, graphics, bullet points and more. Remember it's all about your market and helping them solve their problems.

Headline

Lots of people do not use headlines in their book blurbs, but quite simply, headlines work! Call out to your market with a headline that captures attention. "*How to…*" headlines are easy to create and work very well. Include a big benefit, be specific and – where possible – add an element of curiosity to get your visitors reading more.

It's often good to start by writing out 5 – 10 headlines just to get you started. When you have finished writing your entire sales letter you may come back and discover different angles and unique points. Don't worry too much if your headline isn't very strong when you start writing, you can come back when the blurb is finished and improve it. Personally, I use a great online tool to craft my headlines (see resource list).

Offer

What is your book about and what exactly are you offering your visitors if they buy? Bring out the strongest points in your book and the Unique Selling Point (USP) i.e. what is it that makes your book <u>different</u> to the others? Is it the experience you've got? Maybe your book is more specific, or tackles the biggest hurdles your market experiences?

If you are struggling to identify a USP for your book, then here is a very clever method that has worked for many people and some large companies in the past. List the benefits that your book **and** your competitor's books <u>all</u> offer. Then, find something in that list that is incredibly important to your prospect BUT that your competitors fail to highlight. For example, bleach kills most bugs but only one brand I know of claims that it kills 99% of them dead. I'm pretty sure the others do too, but do they let the public know? Get the idea?

Pricing

Pricing is quite an art in itself, so you should test different prices over the course of time. Whilst you should never aim to compete solely on price, there will be a zone of acceptability within which you can experiment. This is where it (literally) pays you to research your competition and then **test** – yet another aspect of *checking* and *tweaking* – to determine the most effective price point(s) for your product(s).

Above all else, remember that you should price in order to maximise **revenue** (not sales volume) because, as we now know, that is what is of <u>most</u> interest to the *A9 algorithm*. Your sales volume will naturally follow if you get this right, but ensure you price your books to deliver the maximum return because this tactic will move you *up* in the listings.

Sometimes lower prices will convert better and sometimes a higher price will convert best. People often tend to feel that the more they pay, the better the book will be, so an inexpensive book might be seen as 'cheap and nasty' and hence, actually lose sales. On the other hand, the same book with a higher price may be seen as premium. But don't get hung up about the actual sales price. You should always have your eye on the bottom line i.e. <u>revenue</u>, not sales volume, for maximum impact on search results.

This is such an important principle that an example might be helpful, so consider the following carefully. Supposing you had a book priced at ninety nine cents on Amazon, and you were selling just ten copies per month. In that situation, you would be making $3.50 per month in revenue because, on prices of less than $2.99, Amazon pays 35% royalty. Now suppose you were to experiment by increasing your price to the top of the 70% royalty band (where I have four of my non-fiction books positioned at present) to see what happens.

Price	**Vol**	**Revenue**
$0.99	10	3.50
$9.99	2	14.00

If your sales volume for that book were to go *down* to just two books per month as a result, your sales revenue would have actually increased by a factor of four. Now this is just arithmetic, but the important point is this: supposing there were two books in the Amazon store that were on the same subject and were equally well optimised for the same keywords. If one of those books was generating $3.50 per month and the other was generating $14 per month, which of those books do you think the *A9 Algo* is going to push up the listings?

Now just to be clear: I am not saying you should price your book at $9.99 – I am saying that you need to test different price points over the course of time and that you should not worry too much about *sales volume* or your *BSR*. Instead you should be focussed on the MAMM factor that rewards books that consistently deliver the highest revenue. Bottom line is: always price your books in order to maximise revenue. This will push your book higher up in the listings and as a <u>secondary</u> effect increase your sales volume too.

Believability

Good examples of proof are those *before* and *after* pictures you will have seen for weight-loss books. It's even better if they show several people who've all experienced great results. Why? Because it makes your value proposition much more believable. Even if you have exactly the same method as your rivals and even if their book is technically better than yours, if your *proof* is better *you* will make more sales.

So think about the believability factor very carefully when crafting your blurb and think of ways you can you add believability or even proof into your blurb. Have you got evidence of real results? If so, make sure you include it. If you haven't any proof, don't let it hold you back; you can still market and sell your book. As you get customers, you will naturally attract reviews from your buyers which will ultimately provide a degree of social proof.

Bullet points

Again, hardly anyone is using them at present in book blurbs, but your bullet points will be read by lots of readers and sometimes, all it takes is for one bullet point to strike a chord and create an emotional response for you to make the sale.

Your bullet points should include a benefit and perhaps an element of curiosity. The easiest way to write them is by going through your book and pulling out all the best bits. Then turn them into bullet points where you reveal the benefit but not 'how or what to do' – that's how you create curiosity.

A Personal Story

As we have already discussed, stories are something we are wired to tune in to – they generate interest, curiosity and can push emotional buttons. How about the story of the guy who was broke, discovered a system that changed his life and if he could do it, you can too? You are sure to have heard that one. How about the story of the girl with terrible acne, who never had a boyfriend until she found a simple method for perfect skin and now has to turn-down dates?

Best-selling books often have great stories behind them, so you might like to think about including a personal story in your blurb. The fact is that we bond with readers when we're feeling the same pain – its powerful stuff.

How to Get Reviews

As mentioned above, don't let a lack of testimonials or social proof slow you down and stop you getting your book online and selling. Unless your blurb is totally unbelievable, not having these elements may simply reduce your conversions but it won't reduce them to zero.

There are two popular ways to get testimonials, social proof and feedback for your book. The first is to find a group of individuals to review your book. You could email your newsletter list or approach individuals on forums. It's as easy as asking the question: "would you mind reviewing my book and offering me honest feedback?" In many cases, people are more than happy to get a book for free so they can review it. The second popular method is to ask the buyers of your book for feedback. This is often done at the end of a book. It really can really be as easy as asking.

However, my preferred method is to allow reviews to accrue organically. I simply launch and then work on all of the other factors i.e. cover, blurb, price i.e. continually *tweaking* until I get my book selling. After that, the quality and value that I have built in to the offer will speak for itself and reviews will gradually trickle in. Don't be worried about potential negative feedback, simply take it on the chin if, and when it happens which, inevitably, it will at some stage. The feedback from your buyers (even if negative) can be used to update and improve your book, increase buyer satisfaction and generally raise your game.

Blurb Action Step

Get your blurb written right away as soon as you can after your book is finished. Once your listing is live, you can (in theory) begin making sales, so start and finish your blurb in one sitting. Shut the door, turn off your phone and get your first draft up done right away. Read your first draft out loud and tidy up any clumsy sentences and lines. Don't perfect or rewrite it just yet – get it up online.

Over the course of time, continue to improve your conversions by *tweaking* your blurb regularly, following the advice above. You should tweak and test everything but, in particular, tweak your *headlines* and your *prices* whilst you monitor the effect on sales revenue. But remember that there will come a point where the time you spend improving your blurb starts to make little difference to your conversions and, at that point, your time is better spent elsewhere.

Traffic

So, you know your market, you have your book and you have got your blurb created. It's then time to start driving traffic to your book's sales page. There are many different ways to drive traffic but the key is to focus on creating a plan or blueprint you'll be prepared to stick to and follow daily *until* you get things going.

If you're familiar with the 80:20 rule (Pareto's Principle) – how 20% of the things we do get 80% of the results – driving traffic to your listings is the 20% that will yield 80% of the results. Don't misunderstand me here – I am *not* suggesting that you start spending money on advertising. After all, we are in this business to make money; not spend it!

But at least initially, until Amazon takes over the responsibility for you, you do need to start driving traffic and monitoring and improving your conversions. By the way, we are not necessarily talking about achieving *high* sales volume here; we are talking about consistency i.e. regular sales over time. Even if you are generating only one or two sales per month, I promise you that you are going to be doing a whole lot better than the *millions* of authors who cannot sell their work at all! And once you get the ball rolling i.e. you are getting *consistent* sales, the Amazon algo will notice and begin to reward your efforts by multiplying the effect.

Without traffic you will make a big fat zero sales, with traffic you might still make zero sales, but at least now you know you have to work on *conversions* i.e.

your cover and blurb. Bottom line - you <u>need</u> traffic and there are two main types: *free* traffic and *paid-for* traffic, so let's talk about my favourite traffic source, the <u>free</u> kind.

Free Traffic

The best free traffic source for me has undoubtedly been organic search engine traffic from the Amazon search engine itself. That's why we are creating non-fiction books i.e. so we can use *searched-for* keyword phrases in our titles, sub-titles and keyword fields within our listings. However our sales are always going to be limited by the amount of targeted traffic we can get from a keyword search to our book listing.

If only 1000 people are searching for your keyword every month and you're ranking #3 in the Amazon results (SERPS) then you'll only ever get a percentage of 1000 checking out your listing.

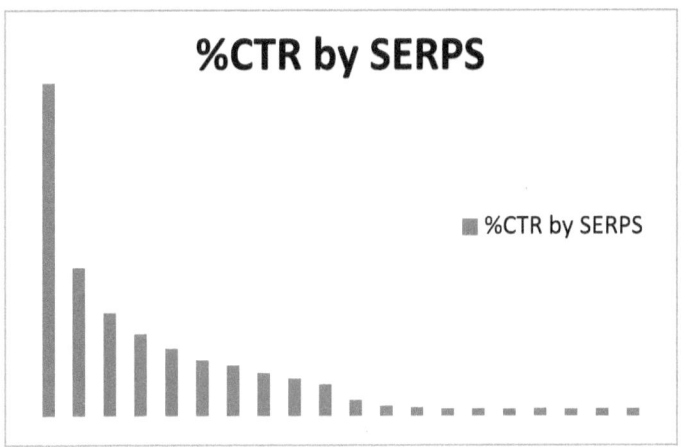

From the above data that I personally aggregated from four different data sources, you can see that the number #1 slot in the SERPS (Search Engine Results Pages) gets about 40% of the search traffic for any given keyword term. But the good news for us is that we can climb the Amazon SERPS by getting our book selling, even if we are selling in low numbers. I cannot emphasise highly enough that you need to get sales at all costs – sales *consistency* will drive you gradually all the way to the top of Amazon's listings.

Bloggers and Affiliates

All niches have busy bloggers talking about their latest findings, gossip and new trends. Blogging (as it was intended to be used) builds a community and is good for the search engines. You can drive traffic to your book listings by working with bloggers. You may like it, you may not feel comfortable with it but it's a fact that the easiest way to put your traffic on autopilot (or at least as close as possible) is by constantly recruiting and motivating other people to do it for you.

You should ideally be looking for bloggers who are also Amazon affiliates. Affiliates specialise in traffic; they don't create offers, they don't have customer support. All they do is drive traffic using a variety of their own preferred methods. Any affiliate worth their salt will have an Amazon Associates (affiliate) account. So find other people who are engaged in building an audience for what you have to offer and then approach them. If you can get bloggers to review your book and link to it via their own Amazon Associates link, they will make money and so will you. At present, my books are being recommended on over eighty different blogs.

One thing that makes Amazon Affiliates very happy indeed is a **low-cost** item that *converts* well and the reason is very simple: the Amazon cookie that is deposited when a visitor clicks an Associate link remains on the visitor's computer for a period of 24 hours thereafter and so **ANYTHING** that person buys from Amazon during that period will earn money for the affiliate!

Fridges, washing machines, garden supplies, movies – hey, I'm not going to list the entire Amazon store here, but hopefully you get the idea. There is an astonishing array of items purchased from Amazon every single minute of every day and an Amazon Associate can earn a hefty commission just by getting their existing traffic to visit Amazon via their affiliate link. Amazon Affiliates love low-cost, *converting* items – such as ebooks. It's not really for the few cents they will make on the book; it's because people are very likely to buy other things too.

Now then, right there I have revealed one of my best kept secrets to you! It can most certainly work for you too if you find the right influencers in your chosen *markets*. But to make it work, you have to do your part! Your cover, blurb, pricing, and ideally, your reviews all need to signal to the prospect that your book is a quality item that they need to purchase. After that, it's just traffic and – as by now you should be appreciating – traffic leads to sales and sales lead to increased visibility in the Amazon listings. But it does not end there because increased visibility leads to even more sales. So we are effectively setting up a virtuous cycle that causes the *A9 Algo* to push you right to the very <u>top</u> of the Amazon listings.

Building Your Empire

When you know people are prepared to spend money on your book, it's time to think about expanding, creating a sales funnel and starting to go deeper.

If you are not already building a list, traffic will be landing on your book listing and those people either buy, or they will not. That's a good place to start, of course, to find out if (and how well) your book converts. Without any delay or 'over thinking' you have your business up and running, you're getting traffic and testing the market as soon as you have your book listed at Amazon. The downside is everyone who doesn't buy leaves your listing and is unlikely to return.

There is no question about it, you are pouring money down the drain unless you build a sales funnel.

Hopefully from the diagram above you'll appreciate that the more people you 'pour' into your funnel (traffic) and the wider the neck at the bottom (conversions) the more money you will make.

As a writer who has chosen to serve the needs of a particular niche, you should be identifying additional opportunities to help people by providing them with more of your products and services. In order for you to contact your buyers in the future, you need to build a list. An email list effectively represents push-button traffic for your future releases. In less than 200 words, by pushing 'send' you can have traffic pouring to any of your offers for days. So, make sure you are always building your newsletter list, keep in touch with your subscribers and build a deepening relationship with them to keep your list active and responsive

The way to build a list is to write something useful and complementary to your book's main subject matter, then give it away in return for a sign-up. I am very sure you will have seen this process in operation on the internet. The page that makes that free offer and contains the sign-up form is technically known as a *lead capture* page and you should put one on your website or blog. The purpose of your lead capture page is to get your visitors onto your list.

Over time, the goal is to build a relationship with the people who sign-up, build trust and constantly remind them about your product offerings. You can interact, ask questions and listen to your prospects. Ask them what their most pressing problems are, what they've tried in the past and what they'd like to try in the future. This is great feedback to help improve your front-end book, *tweak* your sales copy and build your future backend books and services. Get surveys right and you may never have to do a day's niche research ever again.

In addition, provided your products and services are good, you will never have to pay for traffic. If you follow the advice in the previous chapters, Amazon will be sending you a steady stream of visitors and a percentage of those people will buy your book(s). The last thing you need to do is allow your buyers to get away without giving you their contact details. It will be far easier to market to those people in the future if they sign-up for your newsletter..

So make sure your lead-capture page is prominent on your blog or website. Some people even set it as their home page, so important is the process of getting people into your funnel. A good alternative is to have the sign-up form displayed prominently in your sidebar. In addition, have links in all of your books offering the free gift and pointing people to your lead-capture page. Over the course of time you will be building a most valuable asset that can be leveraged over and over again.

Putting It Together

The internet is a funny and frustrating place to be when it comes to setting up an Internet based business. It's sad and it's ironic that when we read the sales page of a brand new book, promising riches, and then we buy, we are buying an information book. Did you get that? We're looking for a solution to our financial worries, so we <u>buy</u> information books, and perhaps miss the truth that *creating* our own books is the real key to success.

It starts by realizing there are no push-button solutions and the surest way to success is by choosing an evergreen business model. One that worked in the past, works today and will work well into the future. You can be different from the 97% of people out there, dreaming and wishing they could change their lives ... by simply watching what other people are doing, taking note and building your own information empire.

Selling information is one of those skills that, once you master it, allows you to work once and get paid over and over again. You can build a residual income, go to bed for 7 hours and wake up richer. Information marketing is an evergreen business model. We'll never satisfy our customer's hunger for information. People will always have problems that cause them pain and they will always be chasing their dreams.

As Lao Tzu said *"The journey of 1000 miles begins with a single step"* your first step is your first book. That's where it all begins, now it's time to stop reading (well nearly) and start applying everything you've learned.

Tips for Getting it Done

Almost every day I get to read a new email about the *#1 Reason for Failure* but right up there – at the top – has to be <u>getting started</u>. Doing something badly will always get better results than doing nothing at all. I don't know anyone not guilty of starting and failing to finish at some stage, so make a commitment to yourself to get your book up, running and selling.

Let me tell you about a fighter called Danny. Man that boy could eat, drink and party like anybody. He could put on over 28lbs after a fight because he's got nothing to train for and nothing to focus on. But when he's got a fight coming up, when he's preparing to throw punches, kicks, knees and elbows at someone (and they're doing their best to hit him back) he trains like a monster. He trains hard, out of necessity to survive the battle of the nerves and the fear of failure in the ring. Maybe you're the same? Late copywriting legend – Gary Halbert - summed it up well in his newsletter.

> "Gun-to-the-head-thinking can get you out of a jam or tough time. If someone held a gun to your head, and to save your life you had to craft the best message you could, what would you say?" – Gary Halbert

Often it's not really the work that's the problem; it's our approach and mind-set towards getting it done. A while back I was listening to an NLP audio by Jason

Fladlien and he was comparing typing to hitting the keys on a cash-register. If you can frame your work differently, perhaps thinking that you're not typing words onto your computer screen, you're actually adding zero's to your bank balance, then maybe you would get a lot more done. Maybe that'll work for you? All it really takes is the right discipline and determination. Tell yourself to turn the TV off and just crack on – you are after-all, your own boss.

Someone once said to me that if I wasn't failing online with some projects then I wasn't pushing hard enough or doing enough. Learning to fail fast is an important part of business. Find an idea and get it up fast. If it fails, then so what? You've not wasted too much time or money on it and you can move on to the next project. Plus you got experience (something no amount of money can buy) and a book you can give away for free as a bonus for future projects – in fact, it's hard to fail when you look at it that way.

Procrastination Killers

"In psychology, procrastination refers to the act of replacing high-priority actions with tasks of low-priority, and thus putting off important tasks to a later time." - Wikipedia

Recently, I bumped into some guy who did a Double-Ironman competition. That's 224 miles on the bike, 4.8 miles swimming and a double marathon (54.4 mile run). It took 40 hours for him to complete it. He talked about the winner to whom he had chatted during the event. The biggest single difference, he said, between the winner and losers was mind-set. The winner got on with it. While everyone struggled up the hills, he just battled through. When asked how he did it, he replied "The quicker I get it done, the quicker I can go home." We're all guilty of checking our emails, spending too much time on Facebook or Twitter and generally wasting time. I know I've spent many an hour 'working' when all I was really doing was reading about working. Just get on with it: the faster you get things done, the faster you'll be enjoying the results.

Time management is a big factor in overcoming procrastination. Stop sitting down for Ironman-like hours on your computer. Instead work solidly for short periods of time – 30 minutes to an hour is fine – then reward yourself with a break. This has the added benefit of putting your unconscious mind to work to come up with solutions and ideas.

Learn to plan your work and then work your plan. Map out your projects, put realistic time frames in place and then stick to them. Once your project is planned, create a weekly and daily plan. Don't find yourself turning on your computer and thinking "What am I going to do today?" That kind of thinking leads to procrastination. You will just be putting off the important stuff that will make you money in the end.

When you sit down at the computer you should know exactly what you have to do, how long you have to do it and then get it done. You sit down with a clear purpose and 'begin with the end in mind.' If you fail to achieve your daily work it's either because you didn't focus or you were unrealistic. Try keeping a diary with a record of what you have to do and the progress you've made. I keep a Notepad file and at the end of each day, update it with what I've done, what I'll do tomorrow and whether or not I've achieved my goals for the day. It's nice to scroll down and read past-entries. It's a little like keeping a food diary. You never realize how bad you've been until you look back and see how many days you ended up being unproductive.

Learn (and have the discipline) to set timescales ... get the work good-enough and then start selling it. This becomes your *Version 1.0*. When your book is selling and you've got feedback from the marketplace you can invest some more time, improve the book and release *Version 1.1, 1.2... 2.0*. Think about all the '*New, Improved*' detergents, toothpastes and recipes released on a regular basis. They're simply newer versions of the same, old thing, improved and re-sold to the same hungry market.

Software firms get this concept and release a version of their program and then release subsequent updates. Sometimes they even release software with bugs they didn't know about until the market tells them, so they fix them and still make millions. Not only is this a quicker way to release your books, it's a great reason to keep in touch with your buyers, interact and ask questions. Then build a super-successful book based on real user feedback.

When you find a hot, hungry market you'll never reach the entire market and you'll never satisfy their desire to consume enough new information. Hot markets are so big there will always be a percentage of people who've never heard of you and want to find out more. How many weight loss DVD's can you think of that teach the same thing perhaps just endorsed by a different celebrity? Of course it's nice to be different, to be unique and be first, but in a hungry market, never let the fact that someone got there first put you off.

Resources

Rather than dotting my recommendations throughout the book, I thought it would be more beneficial to put them all in one handy reference section, so here we go.

Create an account with Kindle Publishing (KDP. Use the information in this guide to create a winning book and then upload it to your Kindle Publishing account. They accept files in many formats including both native both Word format and EPUB. You can set your own pricing and upload your cover graphic. It's completely free and your books gets its own page on the Amazon site.

https://kdp.amazon.com

Hopefully you will already have your own word-processor program, but the free tool Calibre is a must have. It can convert your Word document into EPUB, MOBI (Kindle) and a whole host of other formats. Remember that EPUB is definitely the best format for you to work with.

https://calibre-ebook.com

The program I personally use for market research is *KDP Rocket*. It is an inexpensive tool that you can use to find both niches and keyword phrases to target. It essentially takes away a lot of the guesswork and reports actual search volumes, for both Amazon. But I have recently come across a very good *free* browser extension that does pretty much the same thing.

https://keywordseverywhere.com

For competitor research, you can easily discover the number of actual sales being made by any book on Amazon. Just enter the Amazon BSR (Best Seller Rank) which is show at the bottom of every book listing, into the *free* Jungle Scout tool. Choose which Amazon store you are interested in (you can research different countries), pick 'Kindle Store' (third field) then click the button and the number of actual sales will be shown at the top.

https://www.junglescout.com/estimator/

Universal links are a great way to get your visitors to their preferred bookstore and they also have a reporting feature that tells you how many people actually click your links. If you are planning to publish 'wide' then I recommend that you use these links in your 'about the author' section.

https://www.books2read.com

The job of your headline is to grab attention and get people to start reading your blurb. You should spend time crafting a great headline to improve your conversion rate. Here is an excellent copywriting tool for analysing headlines. It uses a linguistic algorithm based on modelling theory and advertising research.

https://headlines.sharethrough.com

When you are ready to create your own funnel, you will need your own website and autoresponder. For the website, I recommend Wordpress. Essentially, there are two types of Wordpress installation, but getting started with a free account using their own hosting is a very good choice. You can optionally pay for a customised domain with them - this is inexpensive, but not strictly necessary at the beginning.

Create Your Website Here

For your autoresponder, a very good choice is MailChimp. Their free account allows you to create a mailing list of up to 2000 people which is a great way to get started.

https://mailchimp.com

Phew!

That's quite a list, but all of those resources are tools and services that I personally use and can wholeheartedly recommend to you. They will certainly give you an edge over your competition and make the business of getting into profit that much easier.

Finally

Writers block, analysis paralysis, boredom and being overwhelmed are all reasons for not getting your projects finished. If I'm staring at a blank screen wondering what to write and where to start, the best thing (in my opinion) is to simply start writing ... anything. As you type the words will start to flow naturally but first you have to start typing. It's where the magic begins (don't ask me how).

Remember "*write fearlessly and edit ruthlessly.*" It really is the best way to cure writer's block. Just start writing and get your thoughts down then edit and correct your work as a separate process. Prioritise your work. If you've a choice of writing an eBook or formatting the look-and-feel, then write the eBook every time because it's the content that will make you money. If you're wondering whether you should create graphics or get your listing up, then get the listing completed – same reasoning.

Ask yourself "what *should* I do?" Instead of always doing what you want, choose the tasks that deep down, you *know* you should do that will make you money and, nine times out of ten, you'll pick the right task. If you're still not sure, maybe it's a toss-up between two equally important tasks – should I create the book or write the blurb – then give yourself a minute, flip a coin, roll a dice, just pick one but take action. Your income is directly related to the number of books and listings you've got out there and how many people you can get to click on those buttons so remember to get 'em up fast and get to work on driving targeted traffic to your offers. Don't make it more complicated than it is.

Set yourself a goal to create your first book. Treat this as a confidence builder. You will then have your own book to sell or giveaway to build a list and you can then get feedback on it. You can sell it cheaply just to see what the demand is like, how happy your buyers are and discover for yourself that's it's not really that hard. Making your own books is without doubt one of the quickest and easiest ways to start making money online. I can't think of any business easier to set up from home. Anyone can start no matter what your age or level of experience.

A laptop, an internet connection and somewhere comfortable to work – that's all you need. Plan your goals and each day, when you've achieved them, pack up for the day and go do something a little more fun. Living the internet lifestyle is about balance and doing the things you want to *now* and not in 6 months, a year or five years from now. Your internet lifestyle and early retirement can begin right now – don't put it off. The barrier to entry is low, the set-up costs are low and the earning potential is truly unlimited.

Thanks for reading, and good luck my friend.

More from Will Edwards

Born and raised in Liverpool, Will attended the 'tough old school' he wrote about in his first novel *Fergus and Me*. Completing the formal part of his education, he graduated from the University of Birmingham, and travelled the world with the British company Apricot International where he was Technical Manager.

Now enjoying the privilege of being able to write full time, he is committed to producing books that inspire and challenge people to live more rewarding and fulfilling lives. If you enjoyed this book, you are sure to like his other books too; you can get them here:

www.whitedovebooks.com

These days, he lives in a converted old barn nestled into the beautiful Exe Valley in the English county of Devon where he does most of his thinking, walking and writing. In his spare time, he likes to write songs and he can often be seen singing and playing guitar or piano at local musical events.

About White Dove Books

White Dove Books was founded in the year 2000 and was quickly recognized as one of the internet's leading websites for personal development books. We are passionate about personal development and we believe that life holds a specific purpose for you.

Our mission is to help people to develop their own unique talents, abilities and passion in order that they may lead more meaningful, joyful and fulfilled lives.

Copyright © White Dove Books

All Rights Reserved

www.ingramcontent.com/pod-product-compliance
Lightning Source LLC
Chambersburg PA
CBHW030718220526
45463CB00005B/2095